Original title:
The Colors of Paradise

Copyright © 2025 Creative Arts Management OÜ
All rights reserved.

Author: Julian Prescott
ISBN HARDBACK: 978-1-80581-495-5
ISBN PAPERBACK: 978-1-80581-022-3
ISBN EBOOK: 978-1-80581-495-5

Joyous Whispers of the Evergreen

In the forest where giggles bloom,
Trees wear hats of vibrant plume.
Squirrels dance with acorn pride,
While the flowers gossip far and wide.

Bunnies hop in mismatched socks,
Chasing tails like playful clocks.
Laughter spills from every leaf,
As shadows tease the sun's belief.

Frogs in tuxedos croak a tune,
To impress the stars and moon.
Bees wear shades, sipping nectar sweet,
As butterflies tap their happy feet.

In the glade, the fun won't cease,
Nature's jesters never fleece.
With every chuckle, joy's released,
In this land of laughter, never ceased.

Celebrities of the Summer Skies

Clouds act silly, shapes a-flutter,
One's a cat, another's butter.
Sunbeams dance in mirror shades,
While starlings bug the sunshine parades.

Kites are soaring, dressing bright,
Tickled by the winds of light.
Raindrops tap-dance, a joyful pitter,
While crickets sing a tune, a glitter.

Fireflies throw a glittering party,
Lighting up the night, so hearty.
Every twinkle, a wink so sly,
In this playful world, oh my, oh my!

Pigeons strut in feathered flair,
Fashion models without a care.
Summer's stage is set so fine,
As laughter echoes, sip that sunshine!

Traces of a Dreamer's Palette

In a world where socks don't match,
The purple skies begin to hatch.
A chicken winks in shades of green,
While giggling frogs create a scene.

The sun wears stripes of candy canes,
And laughter flows like summer rains.
With painted trees that dance and sway,
Who needs a map to find their way?

Whirlwind of Lush Imagery

There's a rainbow in my cereal bowl,
With glitter flakes to make it whole.
A disco ball floats in the stream,
While marshmallows play hopscotch in a dream.

The daisies wear polka-dots with pride,
As merry-go-rounds spin far and wide.
And every step's a joke in rhyme,
Where giggles bloom and dance with time.

Hues Against the Canvas of Time

A fluffy cloud whispers a joke,
To a purple cow that swiftly pokes.
The sun, a clown with painted shoes,
Tickles the horizon with sunny hues.

Each thought a brushstroke, vivid and bright,
As squirrels juggle acorns just out of sight.
With hugs from rainbows, laughter's the norm,
Where life's a canvas, cheerful and warm.

Sunlit Conversations in Bloom

A sunflower talks to a bumblebee,
About the best spots for afternoon tea.
In a garden dressed in silly hats,
The daisies gossip about the cats.

The wind plays tricks and ties shoes in knots,
As butterflies dance with funny thoughts.
With crayons in hand, I sketch a tune,
Where whimsy reigns beneath the moon.

Ethereal Landscapes Awash with Light

In a field of cotton candy skies,
Lollipops grow tall, oh what a surprise!
Squirrels wearing hats, they strut and prance,
A parade of whimsy in a bright floral dance.

Jellybean trees sway to the breeze,
While marshmallow clouds aim to tease.
A rainbow cat plays a harp of cheese,
And giggles ride on the fluffy knee of ease.

Prism of Exquisite Wonders

Bouncing bubbles filled with laughter,
Chasing giggles, we all go after.
A taffy slide twirls with zest,
While licorice mice hold a cheese-fest.

In the land where sorrows are banned,
Frogs wear boots and dance hand in hand.
Cupcakes fly with sprinkles so grand,
Whirling through fields, a sweet wonderland.

Cascading Petals of Delight

Butterflies spin in tutu skirts,
While flowers gossip in silly flirts.
A river of soda flows so bright,
And laughter echoes through the night.

Dancing on rainbows, we twirl and spin,
Socks mismatched, with quirky grins.
Every hop brings a jiggle and bop,
As jellybeans plop, we just can't stop!

Where Stars Meet Petals

In a garden where wishes drop,
Stars wear shades and maybe a mop.
Moonbeams wink, with a giggle so light,
While daisies racquetball, oh what a sight!

Tooth fairy's trampoline takes flight,
As sunflowers pretend to delight.
A comedy show in the starlit beams,
Petals laugh hard, fulfilling dreams.

Luminous Horizons of Fantasy

In a land where rainbows play,
And giggles chase the clouds away.
The sun wears shades, so bright and bold,
While butterflies do cartwheels, uncontrolled.

Each tree sings songs in silly tongues,
And flowers dance, the roots have sprung.
The rivers flow with fizzy drinks,
While frogs recite their jokester winks.

Enchanted Layers of Whimsy

Gnomes bake pies in silly hats,
While squirrels wear their finest slats.
A mushroom band begins to play,
As rabbits dance with flair all day.

The hills are painted in pastel hues,
With quirky signs for silly views.
Each critter sports a bowtie bright,
As starry nights bring pure delight.

Savoring Sunset's Embrace

Sunsets drip like melted cheese,
While crickets hum a jazzy tease.
The horizon giggles with orange glee,
As night winks back at you and me.

The stars wear hats and shine like mad,
Fluffy clouds no longer sad.
They lounge in twilight's silly glow,
As giggles swirl in evening's flow.

Drenched in Nature's Lullaby

Trees chuckle with the breeze's kiss,
While rivers gurgle with pure bliss.
Flowers wink and nod, so spry,
As nature sings a lullaby.

The moon joins in with silver beams,
While ants parade in twinkly dreams.
Silly shadows dance with flair,
In this wild world beyond compare.

Colorful Echoes in Still Waters

In waters calm, a splash of green,
A fish with shades, so bright, so keen.
It wriggles past a rainbow's grin,
Winking at ducks, with a cheeky spin.

A lily pad that flies away,
Chasing beetles in a playful fray.
With every ripple, laughter grows,
As frogs wear crowns, and joy bestows.

Sunflowers dance when the wind's a-pout,
They twist and turn, and fling about.
While butterflies trade jokes in flight,
Painting the dusk with pure delight.

So let the giggles fill the air,
With colors bright and silly flair.
For in this world of splashes free,
Every hue shares a joke with me.

Journeys through Lush Landscapes

Through leafy trails where wild things roam,
A squirrel juggles nuts, far from home.
He slips and slides on blades of grass,
Cracking jokes as he'll amass.

Past fuchsia bushes, bees do dance,
Waltzing round, they twirl and prance.
One bumps a flower, a petal flies,
It hits a bunny, oh what a surprise!

Clouds wear hats, with wobbly charm,
While snails slide by without a qualm.
A turtle chases shadows down,
Wishing on dreams and wearing a crown.

In this wonderland, laughter grows,
Where every path an echo flows.
With colors bright and silly cheer,
Life's painted joy is crystal clear.

Whispers of Radiant Hues

In twilight's glow, the whispers sing,
Of orange skies and a purple fling.
A parrot mocks a turtle's song,
As crickets join, all echo along.

The roses giggle, their petals sway,
Telling tales of a bright bouquet.
While daisies chuckle at the moon,
Swaying softly, a floral tune.

Bubbles float in a dazzling brew,
As laughter joins the evening hues.
A wiggly worm wears boots too bold,
Making new friends through the stories told.

In this theater of bright displays,
Where colors dance and laugh all day.
Every evening, cheerful and low,
Brings a canvas of laughter's glow.

A Tapestry of Eden

In gardens where the pine trees sway,
A raccoon plays on branches gray.
He steals a berry, ripe and round,
While squirrels giggle off the ground.

The sun spills gold across the leaves,
As grasshoppers plot in their 'thieving' sleeves.
With every hop and twist they make,
They turn a treat into a quake!

Fluffy clouds wear silly hats,
While kittens stalk with little spats.
Beneath the blooms, the critters tease,
Each flower bows, a royal breeze.

In this tapestry of blissful cheer,
Where laughter echoes far and near.
Colors intertwine, a joyful spree,
Life's a playground; come, dance with me.

Mirage of Unseen Colors

In a land where zebras paint,
And elephants wear hats quite quaint.
The sun throws hues on all it knows,
While giggling flowers strike a pose.

A pink giraffe ran through the trees,
Dancing lightly with the breeze.
While fish in bow ties sing and hum,
In this place where rainbows come!

The rivers flow with fizzy drinks,
Which make you giggle, laugh, and wink.
Each cloud's a dog with floppy ears,
That barks out joy and banishes fears.

So if you seek the wild and fun,
Leave your dull gray worries spun.
In this realm where laughter reigns,
Unseen colors break the chains.

An Embrace of Light and Shade

A sunbeam's tickle on a frog,
That croaks the jokes of a lazy bog.
While shadows wear their funky hats,
To dance with squirrels and make them chat.

The trees are umbrellas for the ants,
Who hold their tiny disco dance chants.
Each leaf whispers a secret jest,
In a game of hide-and-seek, they're the best.

A plump cloud floats with a cheeky grin,
Playing peek-a-boo with the sun's bright skin.
In every corner, smiles bloom wide,
As silliness is our shining guide.

So come embrace this lively play,
Where light and shade frolic all day.
Let's paint the air with laughter's song,
In this joyful place where we belong!

Chasing the Whispering Wind

A windy day was feeling spry,
It blew the hats up to the sky.
Chasing whispers like a kite,
In colors that just felt so right.

The dandelions giggled loud,
As breezes danced with fluffy cloud.
Each gust a chuckle, wild and free,
Tickling flowers, oh what glee!

The squirrels wore scarves, oh so chic,
Making fashion statements unique.
Each gust would play a funny tune,
As petals twirled beneath the moon.

So let's run fast and join the wind,
In this laughter where joys rescind.
For every dash and playful spin,
Brings us closer to the grin!

Melodies of the Floral Symphony

In gardens where the flowers wink,
Bees hum tunes while cats all drink.
Petals sway to jazz and blues,
A symphony in sunny hues.

The roses wear their frilly gowns,
While tulips prance like tiny clowns.
Daisies play a piano bright,
Under twinkling, starry light.

The violets sing in lovely keys,
As ladybugs float on the breeze.
Each bloom a note in nature's score,
Creating joy forevermore.

So listen close, embrace the tune,
Let laughter lift you like a balloon.
In this floral orchestra, we find,
Heartfelt music that's truly kind!

Dappled Sunlight on Petals

In a garden where giggles bloom,
Bees wear hats while ants make room.
With flowers dancing, the sun's a clown,
Tickled by breezes, never a frown.

Petals prance in a polka-dot style,
A rainbow so bright, it's hard to compile.
Where the daffodils chuckle with glee,
While a snail slides by, sipping sweet tea.

Butterflies whirl in a silly parade,
As flowers gossip in the sun's warm shade.
Each color a joke that tickles the air,
In this laughter-soaked, vibrant affair.

The Symphony of Shimmering Shades

One banana sings in a citrus band,
With apples and berries, they all take a stand.
A lemon's punchline, in high-pitched glee,
While a peal of laughter bursts from a pea.

The birthday cake's icing is sticky but sweet,
As cupcakes giggle with jiggly feet.
Marshmallows wobble in fluffy delight,
While sprinkles dance 'til the fall of night.

In this fruit fiesta, sheer joy overflows,
With cherries that chuckle and twist in their clothes.
A serenade sung by a wild, fruity crew,
Where colors collide, and the fun's never through.

A Canvas Where Sunsets Meet

A canvas stretched wide for colors galore,
Where purple cows dream and orange cats snore.
The sun is a painter, with smiles to share,
Brushes of laughter, dancing in the air.

Canvas of laughter filled up with dreams,
In a swirl of laughter, or so it seems.
The night starts to giggle, as stars take the stage,
While moons crack jokes, and shadows engage.

Each hue is a chuckle, bursting with cheer,
As the sky tells stories, tickling the ear.
In this colorful mess, come join the spree,
Where laughter and colors live wild and free.

The Palette of Nature's Embrace

With daffodil jokes and tulip tunes,
Nature's playground lights up the dunes.
A palette that splashes in giggles and grins,
Where sunshine and laughter are all it begins.

The trees wear scarves and the ground's got flair,
As squirrels do ballets, twirling in air.
They wear tiny hats made of acorn and bark,
While the daisies giggle, lighting up the park.

Every leaf is a note in this joyful ballet,
As colors sing loud, and they never decay.
In this canvas of winks, where nature's delight,
Is a riot of humor that shines through the night.

Luminescent Journeys

A fruit parade in rainbow hues,
Bananas dancing in bright blue shoes,
Kiwi juggling with a peach so sweet,
Mango tango on the summer street.

Fuchsia clouds and lime green grass,
A polka-dotted frog with quite the sass,
Hopping high on a tangerine,
Chasing sunbeams, oh what a scene!

A purple owl wearing stylish specs,
Hooting puns with trendy flex,
While daisies laugh in the breeze so light,
Petals twirling in a colorful flight.

In this vivid realm, all's a hoot,
Cactus wearing a snazzy suit,
Dancing through a kaleidoscope,
In the land of whims, we laugh and grope.

Serene Landscapes of Light

A sea of mint with bubblegum waves,
Where chocolate dolphins do playful braves,
Cotton candy clouds float by with a twirl,
Spinning colors in a swirl.

Beetroot birds chirp in jolly delight,
Sipping sunshine from morning till night,
While licorice trees sway trends anew,
In this serene land of a caffeine view.

Carrot cake mountains rise wide and bright,
With sprinkles on top, oh what a sight!
Riding rainbows on licorice trails,
With lollipop wind, adventure never fails.

Life's a giggle in pastel trees,
Where jellybeans bounce in the summer breeze,
Each moment sparkles, a vibrant beam,
In hues of happiness, we simply beam.

Festival of Vivid Dreams

Joyful turtles wearing party hats,
Beaches of butter with seagull spats,
Pumpkin spice iguanas sipping cheer,
Giggling softly as the parade draws near.

Cupcake floats in a sea of spritz,
Cookies launching with frosted blitz,
Watermelon bands play funky tunes,
As gumdrops dance under bubble balloons.

A jester fox with a jive so slick,
Cracking jokes with a marshmallow stick,
Fluffy clouds catch the giggles so bright,
In this fair of colors, all feels just right.

Join the jest, let your spirit sway,
In this vivid dance, come what may,
Every shade sings a tune so light,
Embrace the laughter, join in tonight!

Embracing the Spectrum of Life

Sippin' lemonade from a rainbow cup,
With gummy worms that are ready to sup,
The day cascades in colors aglow,
As jellybean buses begin to flow.

Joyous lemons wearing sunny smiles,
Tickling laughs across the miles,
Pineapples twirl with a peachy delight,
In this spectrum, everything feels just right.

Raspberry raindrops tap-dance so sweet,
On fruity sidewalks where candies meet,
With cotton clouds sailing bright and grand,
Every hue crafts a colorful band.

Let's paint the world with sparkles gold,
And laugh together, let life unfold,
In this playful canvas, we thrive and kite,
With vibrant dreams bringing pure delight.

Celestial Brushstrokes

In the sky, a painter grins,
Throwing blues at fluffy skins.
Orange giggles under suns,
While clouds wear hats and silly buns.

There's a rainbow, sipping tea,
With purple spoons and sweet esprit.
Each color tosses jokes around,
As laughter echoes, joy is found.

From violet to a sunny cheer,
The hues all dance and crank up gear.
They tickle rain and swirl in mist,
With brush and canvas, they can't resist.

So grab your palette, paint the day,
In silly shades, let colors play.
Laugh along, it's quite a spree,
In this wacky, bright jubilee.

Harmony in Chromatic Delights

A yellow duck sings high and sweet,
With pink balloons that dance, compete.
Green grass tickles legs that prance,
While silly socks join in the dance.

Blueberries giggle and throw pies,
As lemonade winks with surprise.
The orange sun trips on a beam,
In this zany and bright daydream.

Red roses wear comical hats,
Complaining to nearby acrobats.
The colors blend without a care,
In a world that's light and rare.

So let's embrace this painted spree,
With laughter and a jubilee.
In harmony, we'll paint the night,
With colors that tickle pure delight.

Eden's Kaleidoscope

At dawn, the flowers play charades,
In hues of jest, where nothing fades.
The daisies laugh, the tulips giggle,
As ladybugs all dance and wiggle.

Apples sprout with polka dots,
While monkeys juggled, oh, what plots!
A chromatic breeze blows through the chairs,
As colors tease out all their flares.

The rainbow throws confetti wide,
Where giggles flourish, dreams abide.
Each splash of color has a quirk,
In this Eden's dazzling perk.

So paint your life with tones of cheer,
Invite the world to gather near.
In this kaleidoscope of light,
We laugh and dance through day and night.

Prisms of Infinite Wonder

A prism splits the sun's bright grin,
And out it spills—oh, what a spin!
Riddles of colors twist and play,
Creating mischief throughout the day.

The orange cat climbs like a pro,
On a line of purple, stealing the show.
Green bubbles float with giddy charms,
While light holds all in joyful arms.

Spectacles dance on the grass so green,
The insects giggle in a twirling scene.
With every hue, they start to prance,
In this odd, colorful romanced dance.

Let laughter spread like paint on walls,
Embrace the joy, hear the calls.
For in this wonder, bright and funny,
Life's a canvas, always sunny.

Radiant Souls Intertwined

In a world where socks can clash,
Bright pink with stripes that dash,
Laughter spills from every fold,
As vibrant tales of fun unfold.

A purple cat hops on the train,
With polka dots, it's not insane,
It winks and plays with fiery zest,
Where colors laugh and never rest.

The trees wear hats of neon green,
Waving hands in a silly scene,
Sunshine giggles through beams of glare,
In this place, no one has a care.

From bubblegum to sunny gold,
Every creature is quite bold,
Life's a riot with hues so bright,
Painting joy from morning to night.

Fragments of Paradise's Brush

Brush dipped in jellybean delight,
Paints the world in colors bright,
A dancing frog with silly shoes,
Wahoo, it grooves to funky blues.

Granite grins in pastel shades,
As giggling flowers throw parades,
Bouncing bunnies in plaid attire,
Sparkling sparks of joyful fire.

Marshmallow clouds just love to tease,
Painting rainbows with a sneeze,
A kite in plaid that soars up high,
Chasing sunshine in the sky.

With a wink, the sun says 'hey',
While colors twist and swirls and play,
In this kooky canvas grand,
Every laugh is simply planned.

Dance of Dreamlike Hues

Twirling hues in wild ballet,
Splashing antics that will sway,
A blue giraffe with jokes to spare,
Winks at you from mid-air stare.

Lemon drops and licorice rains,
Watch them dance across the lanes,
Rusty red and teal collide,
In this frolic, let's confide.

A disco ball made out of cheese,
Dropped from heights that spark with ease,
Bouncing beats that make us grin,
Join the fun and let's begin.

Jumping beans and candy skies,
Here, even clouds can win the prize,
With whirlwinds of laughter and cheer,
This wild ride brings us all near.

Where Every Shade Tells a Story

Cyan whispers tales of cheer,
As a clownfish jogs near the pier,
Tickling pinks and oranges laugh,
Painting rainbows in a gaffe.

A polka-dotted elephant spins,
Twirling through these gleeful wins,
Hues of laughter fill the air,
With every splash, we lose our care.

Lavender frogs with cupcakes dance,
While candy-coated breezes prance,
Every shade a chuckle brings,
In this world where laughter sings.

Through every twist and vibrant turn,
In this realm, let's laugh and learn,
For every color has its part,
In carving joy into the heart.

Vivid Echoes of Bliss

In a land where laughter reigns supreme,
Giggling flowers dance, what a dream!
Bumblebees hum with silly tunes,
While rabbits wear hats and strut like tycoons.

Chirping birds share jokes in the air,
As squirrels debate if they're bold or rare.
The sun's a great jester, playful and bright,
Telling tall tales till the fall of night.

Cobalt Skies and Golden Fields

Under skies painted in vivid blue,
The cornfields chuckle, what joy they brew!
Sunflowers wink with a cheeky grin,
While carrots play tag with a mischievous spin.

In this patchwork quilt of gleeful sight,
Worms wear visors, avoiding the light.
Laughter erupts from the tiniest sprout,
As farmers dance, shedding all doubt.

Whirls of Exotic Charm

In jungles where monkeys prank without pause,
Parrots drop puns, giving all a cause.
Chameleons change with the silliest flair,
While lizards compete for the best wig they're wear.

Bananas slip on the ground with delight,
Causing giggles as they take a flight.
Tropical breezes hum tunes so absurd,
In a waltz with the trees, it's simply unheard!

The Glow of Abundant Life

In a meadow where joys come to play,
Fireflies twinkle as if to say,
Double the giggles, double the cheer,
Sparkles of laughter dance through the sphere.

Even grasshoppers join the fun-filled scheme,
Jumping in rhythm, living the dream.
Nature's a stage, and oh what a sight,
As critters unite under the moonlight!

Surreal Fields of Bloom

In fields where socks and shoes take flight,
Gnomes dance wildly, what a sight!
The daisies giggle, the roses cheer,
While bunnies hop with nary a fear.

A purple cow walks by with grace,
Sipping tea while wearing lace.
The sun wears shades, all cool and bright,
As butterflies zoom past in delight.

The ants throw parties, donuts galore,
While ladybugs sing, asking for more.
Grasshoppers play tunes on tiny flutes,
While daisies don their snazzy suits.

Oh, the mischief this land has spun,
Where every patch tells of silly fun.
So come and join this riotous play,
In fields of bloom where laughter stays.

Dreamscapes Laced with Light

In dreamland where candy clouds drift high,
A marshmallow sun beams in the sky.
Cats wear hats with feathers galore,
While squirrels debate on who's keeping score.

Rainbow rivers flow with chocolate streams,
As fish recite the silliest memes.
The trees talk gossip, their leaves a-flutter,
While unicorns giggle and snort with sputter.

Puppies prance, on pogo sticks,
While waffles play chess with clever tricks.
The moon does a jig, the stars cheer loud,
As dreams unfold where nonsense is allowed.

So drift on pillows, join this bright night,
In dreamscapes laced with pure delight.
Where silly wonders never grow old,
And laughter's the magic, bright and bold.

Blissful Chromatics

In a place where colors spin around like tops,
Jellybeans rain from candy shop crops.
A teal octopus plays hopscotch with flair,
While green apples juggle without a care.

Clouds made of cotton candy popcorn,
As candy canes grow in bushes of thorn.
Fruit bats wearing shades flip in the air,
While turtles stroll with a casual flare.

Elephants paint rainbows on trees,
While crickets laugh at the buzzing bees.
Chameleons dress in striped plaid pants,
While hippos practice their latest dance.

Oh, the joy that this land can elicit,
Where chuckles and giggles are simply exquisite.
In blissful chromatics, come see the thrill,
Where whimsy's the rule, and time stands still.

Murmurs of the Spectrum

In a world where whispers are rainbow hues,
The fish in the pond sing the silliest blues.
The rocks play tag, oh what a jest,
While frogs in tuxedos look quite impressed.

The clouds wear sneakers, bouncing for fun,
As the sun plays pranks, oh what a pun!
Grass tickles toes as laughter erupts,
While squirrels throw pies, they're all disrupted.

Glittering stars wear party hats bright,
Plans for a ball, oh what a delight!
Fireflies twirl with sparks in their dance,
While hedgehogs groove in a comical trance.

So swirl with the murmurs, join in the cheer,
Where giggles abound, and joy is quite near.
In the spectrum of fun, let your spirit play,
For laughter's the brush that colors the day.

Dances of Vibrant Nights

Under the moon, the colors prance,
A purple chicken starts to dance.
The stars giggle, if you peer hard,
As fireflies flash their glowing card.

The trees wear wigs made of bright thread,
While gopher bands spin tunes in their head.
The crickets croon in pitchy tones,
As night slips in with glittery loans.

Old raccoons twirl in polka shoes,
While owls debate the latest news.
They juggle acorns with charming flair,
And squirrels join in with jazz hands, I swear!

So come join in, don't hesitate,
This circus of hues won't wait!
With every note and every shade,
A giggling night parade is made.

The Glimpse of Dawn's Canvas

As dawn rolls in, the sun goes splat,
Creating hues that make you chat.
Clouds wear pink like a puffy coat,
Sipping coffee from a skyward boat.

A little bird sings off-key tunes,
While rabbits hop on floating moons.
Each blade of grass owns its own shade,
While flowers giggle in their parade.

The bees wear shades, cool and chic,
With tiny hats, they buzz and sneak.
A donut sun rolls down the sky,
As pancake clouds flip by, oh my!

So grab a brush, let colors swim,
Each dawn's a laugh, each light's a whim.
In this zany world, just run wild,
And paint away, like a happy child.

Where Light Meets Bloom

In gardens bright, where colors clash,
A sunflower dreams of a fashion flash.
The daisies giggle, their skirts so wide,
As tulips twirl on a joy-filled ride.

Butterflies wear their best tuxedos,
While bumblebees throw sweet-bravados.
The violets laugh, full-on delight,
As day drips in, a sweet palette of light.

Colors mix in a swirling scheme,
With poppy red and minty cream.
The daisies, dandy, prance and tease,
With honey drips from the buzzing bees.

Where light dances on every petal's tip,
Is where the giggles never slip.
So join the fun, don't let it fade,
In this cheerful bloom parade.

A Symphony of Thriving Shades

The chorus sings in shades of green,
While lizards skate on a leafy scene.
Our colors join, a quirky band,
In harmony that's oh-so-grand.

Marigolds compete with a hearty cheer,
While daisies spin, drawing near.
A tangerine frog leaps with delight,
As colors dance through day and night.

Each shade whispers silly stuff,
Creating mixes that are just enough.
So shake a leg, don't sit and mope,
In this symphony of rainbow hope.

With laughter ringing; a vibrant show,
Where every color gets to glow.
Join the fiesta, bright and bold,
As shades of laughter joyfully unfold.

A Garden of Chromatic Delights

In a garden where zebras roam,
Sunflowers wear hats made of foam.
Chickens dance in polka-dot shoes,
While shy bunnies play peekaboo blues.

There's a tree sprouting jellybeans,
And rain clouds that drip fudgey creams.
The bees hum tunes of silly delight,
As butterflies play tag, oh what a sight!

Ladybugs sporting such vibrant shades,
Share secrets with chipmunks, in leafy glades.
Giggling grapes roll down the hill,
As laughing eyes twinkle and thrill.

Here, even the toadstools paint the scene,
Dressed up in stripes of pink and green.
It's a wacky, whirly, giggly spree,
In a garden bursting with whimsy glee.

Vibrant Echoes of Bliss

In skies of paper-mâché blues,
Squirrels wear sunglasses, sipping on brews.
Cactus wear tutu skirts, so proud,
While silk-worms recite poems, quite loud.

Each flower a character, bold and bright,
Dandelions shoot wishes on a kite flight.
Grasshoppers play hopscotch on beams,
While dragonflies sizzle, cooking up dreams.

The sun winks down with mischievous glee,
As frogs in bowties shout 'Look at me!'
A snail dressed in gold rushes past,
Squeaking with laughter, oh what a blast!

This place glimmers with zany delight,
Where colors twirl in a dance of light.
Each moment a tickle, each hour a tease,
In the land of vibrant echoes, full of ease.

The Palette of Heavenly Sights

There's a rainbow that wears a mustache,
And a moonbeam with a penchant to flash.
Clouds chuckle softly, rolling like cats,
While stars dress in ties and floppy hats.

Each sunset is a giggle parade,
With colors that dance, not afraid.
Crickets croon in harmony sweet,
Providing a soundtrack for the fleet.

Eagles perched on high trees sat,
Wearing party hats in this merry chat.
Lollipops grow from the grass, how neat!
While puppies spin in silly heat.

The horizon hums a whimsical tune,
While tulips flirt with the cheeky moon.
In this place where laughter takes flight,
Life is a carnival, pure delight.

Blooming in Technicolor

In fields where rainbows tumble and roll,
Flowers tickle toes on a stroll.
Pansies gossip, wearing bright caps,
While daisies share naps with giddy chaps.

The sky's an artist with a large brush,
Painting clouds in an outrageous hush.
Worms play chess in the soil below,
While roses boast, putting on a show.

Pigs wear ribbons, winking at sheep,
As the sun spills laughter in a heap.
Everything giggles in the warm breeze,
Even the branches sway with ease.

At dusk, wonder shines in every hue,
Where colors clash in a grand debut.
Each petal and leaf a jester's spree,
In a world bursting with kitschy glee.

Singing in Technicolor

In a land where laughter flows,
And squirrels wear tiny clothes,
Rainbows dance on cotton candy,
With flavors that are far from dandy.

The sun slips on a polka-dot hat,
While turtles do the cha-cha chat,
Bluebirds take the stage with flair,
Each note tickles the air with care.

A frog in boots leads the parade,
With clumsy moves, he isn't afraid,
They juggle pies and jelly beans,
Creating chaos like silly scenes.

With giggles bursting in every hue,
Bubbling giggles, oh what a view!
Together they sing, a goofy crew,
In a world where joy is always new.

Fragments of Celestial Delight

Balloons float past like silly dreams,
Unicorns giggle, or so it seems.
Stars wear sunglasses, shining bright,
While moonbeams giggle, pure delight.

Candy clouds swirl and twist around,
Sprinkling laughter on the ground,
A babbling brook skips rocks for fun,
While fireflies dance till day is done.

A cat in stripes plays piano tunes,
While fish in hats sing to the moons,
Each moment bursts with playful vibes,
In this land where humor thrives.

With snickers and chuckles filling the air,
Every corner packed with flair,
Fragments of joy, in cosmic play,
In a universe of laughs each day.

Blossoms Beneath an Azure Dream

Petals giggle with colors so bright,
While bumblebees dance in pure delight.
Roses wear glasses; tulips wear hats,
As daisies perform acrobat chats.

The sky paints whispers of giggly sighs,
A butterfly winks, oh what a surprise!
Bees play tag with scents on the breeze,
Tickling flowers like silly tease.

Under blooms, the critters all play,
Dancing to drums made of hay,
Chasing rain with silly grace,
In this vibrant, joyful space.

Laughter sprouts in every nook,
As butterflies plot like an open book,
In this garden, bright and bold,
Stories of smiles and fun unfold.

A Reverie in Emerald Tones

In a meadow where giggles sprout,
Frogs wear crowns and stars sing out.
The grass tickles toes, just like a tease,
While bees sip nectar with utmost ease.

Lizards perform in dazzling attire,
Twirling and whirling with playful fire,
Each joyous note brings a sunny jam,
As turtles cheer, woefully glam.

The leaves whisper secrets in Hula-hoops,
While wiggly worms giggle in loops,
With sprightly hops and stretchy flair,
Engaging in the silliest affair.

In emerald hues, laughter is spun,
Under the sky, there's so much fun,
Where quirky dreams come out to play,
And nonsense rules the joyful day.

Vibrant Visions of a Cherished World

In a land where rainbows play,
Lollipops grow day by day.
The sun wears sunglasses bright,
And giggles take to flight.

Cows paint spots on every wall,
While dancing goats begin to crawl.
With jellybean trees that sway,
A sweet surprise on every play.

Pigs wear hats and scream with glee,
On bouncy clouds, we drink sweet tea.
Where every laugh's a silly song,
In this world, we all belong.

At twilight, stars start to glow,
As marching ants put on a show.
With pastel skies that stretch so wide,
Come join the fun, let dreams collide!

Mosaic of Enchanted Dreams

Where gumdrops line the streets and roam,
And rhyming squirrels call it home.
The sky's a canvas, splashed with fun,
As giggles chase the setting sun.

Ducklings wear a tux and dance,
While squirrels engage in silly prance.
Each flower beams with painted faces,
As laughter fills all the spaces.

A jellyfish takes a stroll in style,
With jellybeans that make you smile.
In wonderlands of pastel hues,
Life spills over, bright with news.

So grab some friends and take a seat,
Join the parade of tasty treats.
The magic's real, let's not delay,
In this land where fun's the way!

Radiance of Forgotten Gardens

In gardens where the daisies dance,
Bumblebees wear lids for their romance.
Tulips giggle when winds blow,
In shades of neon, joy will grow.

Lemonade rivers flow with zest,
While butterflies wear vests, oh, the best!
Sunshine sprinkles laughter wide,
In a picnic of dreams we slide.

Frogs sing opera, suave and bold,
In leafy greens, secrets told.
With a hint of mint in the air,
This charming world is beyond compare.

As night settles in with sparkly glee,
Stars play chess with honey bees.
Join the laughter, let's take a peek,
In gardens where antics reach their peak!

Infinity in the Blooming Sky

Above the clouds where kites collide,
With giggly clouds that jump and slide.
A rollercoaster made of rain,
Twists and turns without the strain.

Marshmallow hills and chocolate streams,
All float on laughter, bursting dreams.
The sun sings songs of candy flare,
As fluffy critters leap with flair.

Where popcorn fields get wild and loud,
And uproarious dance parties draw a crowd.
The breeze is filled with silly jokes,
As balloons burst with playful pokes.

At dusk, the fireflies bring their cheers,
Lighting up the world with giggles and tears.
In this whimsical place up high,
Join the fun that never says goodbye!

Tranquil Shades of Bliss

In a garden where giggles bloom,
And painted snails dance with great boom,
The sky wears polka dots of glee,
While happy trees sip their joyful tea.

A butterfly misplaces its flight,
Chasing shadows that twirl with delight,
Bees wear hats made of sunflower fluff,
Sipping nectar that's way too tough.

In this land where laughter sets the pace,
Clouds do summersaults; it's quite the race,
Rabbits don sunglasses, oh what a sight,
As they hop on rainbows, feeling just right.

Under a sun that tickles the cheeks,
Each breeze brings whispers of silly tweaks,
Here joy spills out like a candy jar,
In tranquil shades, we shine like a star.

Reflections in a Dreaming Pool

In a pond where turtles wear bow ties,
Frog choirs sing with their goofy cries,
Ducks in ballet shoes take a spin,
While fish debate who'll win the swim.

Mirrors ripple with every splash,
As leaves giggle in a leafy clash,
The moon wears a hat made of cheese,
While fireflies play follow the breeze.

A sleeping cat dreams of hovering pies,
While ants find treasure beneath the skies,
Squirrels tell tales of their grand heists,
As the water shimmers with nature's feasts.

Here in this pool, the world is bright,
Where laughter dances in sheer delight,
Every reflection hints at cool cheer,
In a whimsical realm that feels so near.

Woven Dreams in Subtle Colors

In a tapestry spun with giggles and cheer,
Clouds knit dreams, both bright and dear,
Colorful threads, a whimsical spree,
Stitching joy, oh can you see?

A cat with a hat sings a silly tune,
While shadows sway beneath the moon,
Each stitch whispers secrets and rhymes,
In our colorful world where fun climbs.

Grinning flowers wave with delight,
As butterflies wear shoes oh-so-tight,
Bees play hopscotch on the green blades,
Every corner is filled with playful jade.

In this woven realm, we skip and twirl,
Painting our stories with a carefree swirl,
As laughter lingers in vibrant plight,
Crafting a day that feels just right.

Harmonies of Nature's Imprint

In a world where crickets compose tunes,
And rabbits beat drums with their boons,
Nature's laughter fills the air,
As squirrels dance in a carefree flair.

The sky strums strings of pastel light,
While flowers hum songs of pure delight,
Every breeze plays tag with the trees,
As giggles scatter like fallen leaves.

Here sunshine sprinkles the ground in cheer,
And every echo loves to draw near,
Blending sounds of joy, each sweet hint,
In this harmony, happiness glint.

With melodies swirling, we spin and sway,
In a playground of colors where we play,
Together we dance on this joyful sprint,
In nature's embrace, we leave our imprint.

A Dazzling Garden of Wishes

In the garden, flowers dance,
Wishing wells with every prance.
Tulips giggle, daisies play,
As butterflies join their ballet.

Sunflowers with their giant grins,
Compete for laughs, and no one wins.
Roses tell puns, blush in delight,
While violets plot silly kite fights.

Laughter sprinkles on the grass,
Bumblebees buzz, they don't let it pass.
Even the weeds wear silly crowns,
Waving to the sun like clowns.

In this garden, joy will sprout,
With every joke, there's no doubt.
A dazzling world where wishes bloom,
And every petal chases gloom.

Surreal Blossoms in Full Bloom

In a dream where colors twirl,
Petals giggle in a swirl.
Guided by the wind's soft song,
Every blossom hums along.

A violet wears a funky hat,
Daffodils dance, jumping like a cat.
Chasing shadows, chasing rays,
In this place, we laugh for days.

Marigolds cook up a feast,
With herbs and spices, oh what a beast!
But their soup always tastes like grass,
Yet everyone still raises a glass.

These surreal sights, oh, so bright,
Where every day feels just right.
Blossoms tease the morning sun,
In this world, we all have fun.

Symphony of Nature's Prism

A rainbow slipped on a banana peel,
It landed in a daffodil reel.
From orange to blue, they all take stage,
In this symphonic color rampage!

Conducted by the chirping birds,
Where laughter dances, no need for words.
The trees sway to the leafy tune,
And even mushrooms join the swoon.

Grasshoppers hop on marching beats,
While ants juggle tiny treats.
A turtle's slow and silly glide,
Makes everyone laugh, "What a ride!"

In this concert of delight,
Nature performs day and night.
The prism shines, it's all a game,
In this symphony, never the same.

Echoes of Colorful Dawn

As dawn paints skies in hues so bright,
Birds wake up, ready for flight.
The sun's a giant, baked-in pie,
Making each morning laugh and cry.

Clouds wear pajamas, fluffy and white,
Chasing the sun, avoiding a bite.
While flowers stretch, yawning wide,
As night's colorful dreams subside.

A rainbow slips through morning's door,
Tickling petals with colors galore.
While bumblebees start their busy buzz,
In this dawn, every heart just fuzz.

Echoes of laughter fill the air,
As colors and giggles dance everywhere.
In this vibrant, silly light,
Morning sings, and all feels right.

Twilight in the Radiant Realm

In the land where giggles grow,
The sky wears socks, a vibrant show.
Trees dance in polka-dot delight,
While butterflies bounce in neon flight.

Silly rabbits wear tiny hats,
And sing with joyful acrobat cats.
The brook giggles as it flows,
Tickling pebbles in rainbow throws.

Dancing clouds with candy canes,
Whispering secrets, playing games.
The stars wink in silly glee,
While frogs croak a croaky spree.

Oh, to frolic in this daft scene,
Where even the veggies are dressed in green!
With laughter swelling like sweet cream,
In this twilight, we all daydream.

Canvas of the Celestial Garden

In a garden where colors collide,
Painting petals with laughter as they glide.
Bees wearing sunglasses buzz through the air,
Chasing after daisies with flamboyant flair.

The carrots have smiles, the lettuce can dance,
Making me giggle at every chance.
Tomatoes throw parties under the moon,
While pumpkins waltz to a funky tune.

Rainbows sprinkle confetti from the sky,
As kites shaped like birds somehow fly by.
In this garden, silliness reigns,
Where even the soil crackles with gains.

Unicorns paint the fence with their tails,
While pickles chat about epicails.
Each moment here is one of mirth,
A canvas of joy, a treasure of worth!

Fusion of Nature's Warmth

When sunbeams giggle and tickle the leaves,
The world transforms in whimsical weaves.
A squirrel in shades strikes a pose,
Offering us nuts from his stylish clothes.

Flowers wear shoes of glittery lace,
As the breeze plays tag, moving with grace.
The sun's a jester, casting bright rays,
Lighting up laughter in comical ways.

Clouds serve popcorn, fluffy and bright,
While crickets serenade into the night.
Rabbits team up for a grand ballet,
Each hop and twirl makes the flowers sway.

Oh nature's warmth is a playful game,
Full of surprises that never seem tame.
With chuckles and giggles, we frolic around,
In the heart of this magic, joy can be found.

Shades of Utopian Whispers

In a land where laughs are painted in blue,
Squirrels debate on the best shade too.
Sunflowers chant in a quirky tune,
While crickets wear hats that look like a moon.

Giggling glades full of silly trees,
Sing songs of joy swaying in the breeze.
Each leaf a dancer, each twig a clown,
Spreading good vibes all over the town.

Stars sprinkle giggles in the twilight air,
With mischievous winks, they spark a dare.
Fireflies flicker with zany grins,
Inviting us out—come join in their spins!

This whimsical realm offers delight,
With shadows that twirl and colors so bright.
In these playful whispers, we find our cheer,
In shades of laughter, we hold dear.

Hues of Tranquil Moments

In a garden of socks, blue and green,
Where gnomes dance a jig, unseen.
The sun wears a hat made of cheese,
While bees trade puns with the swaying trees.

Purple marshmallows float in the air,
While squirrels gossip without any care.
A rainbow rolls down like a big slide,
And laughter erupts from the colors aside.

The clouds all wear sunglasses, quite bold,
As kittens in tutus do pirouettes gold.
Each shade tells a joke with a wink and a grin,
In this whimsical world, let the fun begin!

Join in the fun, let your worries depart,
In hues that will tickle your light-hearted heart.
With each splash of color, a giggle ignites,
As joy paints the canvas of playful delights.

Fragments of Blissful Light

A banana phoned me, dressed in bright pink,
It asked for some jelly, oh what do you think?
Sunflowers wear sneakers, they're ready to race,
While kittens with spatulas juggle with grace.

Cotton candy clouds tickle a laughing sun,
As flowers with faces play hide and seek fun.
The river's a giggle, it bubbles and bounces,
In puddles of color, the laughter announced.

Marshmallow trees sway with a chuckle or two,
And snails tell tall tales while sipping on dew.
Each ray is a dancer, spinning with glee,
In this joyful domain, gracefulness is key.

Let's waltz with the colors, skip, hop and twirl,
Each fragment of light makes your heart do a whirl.
In this silly spectrum, nothing's quite right,
But joy fills the air, in fragments of light!

The Language of Blooming Colors

A purple elephant wrote me a note,
Inviting me over for the best goat float.
The daisies all giggle, with petals so bright,
While butterflies argue 'bout who takes the flight.

Green apples dance on ridiculously tall chairs,
As a rainbow pizza gets served with great care.
Chirping crickets recite poetry sweet,
While fireflies glow to the whimsical beat.

Pineapple curls on a flamingo's head,
As laughter erupts in a flowerbed spread.
Each color's a word, spinning tales of delight,
In this vibrant affair, everything feels right.

Let's speak in the shades that tickle our soul,
With laughter and whimsy, let laughter take hold.
In this language of beauty, we dance and we sing,
With blooming expressions, our joy takes to wing!

Kaleidoscope of Joyful Horizons

The sun wears a tutu, it's quite the sight,
While giggles erupt from the ladybug flight.
A jellybean cloud drips sugar with style,
And ants host an orchestra, a colorful dial.

In a realm of odd hats, all shapes and sizes,
The trees tumble over in funny disguises.
A silver fish juggles, just out of reach,
While daisies take turns to teach all they preach.

With laughter as our compass, we sail through the day,
In a world made of winks, where silliness sways.
Each moment a snapshot of whimsy and cheer,
As colors collide, creating joy far and near.

Catch a glimpse of the humor painted in hues,
With each kaleidoscope twist, it's laughter we choose.
Let's ride on the waves of this colorful quest,
In horizons of joy, we are truly blessed!

Whispers of Radiant Blooms

In fields where pinky daisies dance,
A bumblebee forgot his pants.
The tulips laugh, they can't believe,
A flowered world that's hard to leave.

The sun wears shades, a silly sight,
While daisies twirl beneath the light.
They gossip sweetly, in the breeze,
About the roses' smelly sneeze.

A daffodil tells jokes galore,
While dad's lawn gnomes plot for more.
Beneath the arch of rainbows bright,
The petals wink in sheer delight.

So come and join this floral spree,
Where jesters bloom on every tree.
In this garden, laughter looms,
And every bud is full of zooms.

Spectrum of Serene Dreams

Where oranges spill and grapes take flight,
A cantaloupe wore socks, oh what a sight!
The spinach sings an off-key tune,
While carrots compete under the moon.

The lettuce waltzes, dressed in green,
It dreams of being a maraschino bean.
Tomatoes giggle in their red hue,
"Let's ketchup!" they yell, "To the garden crew!"

Chasing clouds on candy-floss trails,
Where purple eggplants tell silly tales.
A broccoli crowns a lively king,
Proclaiming jesters bring the zing!

Beneath the skies of fruity cheer,
Every seed whispers, "Laughter's near!"
In this fruity patch, fun gleams bright,
With every sunrise, joy takes flight.

A Tapestry of Eden's Hues

In fields where peacocks prance undeterred,
A quirky goat sings, oh so absurd.
The tulip hats dance, quite a sight,
As daisies gossip, fully polite.

Tickled by breezes, the flowers play,
While ladybugs prance in bright dismay.
A sunflower bows, takes a grand bow,
While clovers giggle, "We've won, and how!"

Rainbow ribbons curl in the air,
Where every bloom sings without a care.
The bees wear shades, and buzz with style,
In this garden, laughter walks a mile.

Let's sip on nectar, a funny brew,
Where every moment feels brand new.
In this patch of hues that dance and sway,
Life is a joke that's here to stay!

Lush Vistas of Joy

In meadows where wild onions play,
A squirrel spins tales in a silly way.
The daisies twirl in polka-dot socks,
While frogs wear crowns made from old rocks.

A swinging vine tickles every nose,
As the grasshoppers wear fancy clothes.
While lilacs laugh with a gentle sway,
The daisies tease the clouds above, so gray.

Fruit flies join in a dance so grand,
As pie charts are drawn in the sandy land.
The wind blows soft, with a chuckle or two,
In this lush vista, where fun is the glue.

So frolic along, where joy blooms wide,
With each little zany, misshapen slide.
In this garden of giggles, let all rejoice,
For every petal has a funny voice.

Spectrum of Serenity

A yellow duck in a blue pond,
Sipping tea and feeling fond.
A green frog wears a tiny hat,
Jumping around, oh, how quaint is that!

Red ants dance, all in a row,
While a snail takes it nice and slow.
Purple butterflies flutter and sway,
Chasing giggles before they play.

Orange sunsets turn into pies,
While pink clouds whisper silly lies.
The spectrum gleams with a shiny grin,
In a land where nonsense wears a pin.

So laugh with me in this fruity haze,
Where every hue sets laughter ablaze.
A palette of joy, a wild delight,
In this funny show, we take flight!

Blossoms in a Vibrant Dream

Petals giggle in electric hues,
A tickling breeze stirs up some muse.
Carrots don hats, melons play tricks,
In a garden where nonsense picks!

Daisies sing with a funky beat,
While bunnies breakdance on their feet.
Purple grapes throw a wild bash,
As squirrels join in, full and brash.

Tulips in top hats, looking quite grand,
Shuffle and sway, taking a stand.
In this vibrant dream, nothing's too silly,
When daisies and carrots dance all willy-nilly!

So join this party, no need to nap,
With flowers in laughter, we're caught in a trap.
A bouquet of giggles, a crop full of cheer,
With blossoms that tickle, come join us here!

Paintings of Ecstasy

In the gallery of giggles and hues,
Splashing paint on everything we choose.
An elephant twirls in bright polka dots,
While fish wear glasses, connecting the spots.

A rainbow giraffe winks with a wink,
As squirrels sip orange juice without a blink.
The canvas swirls in hilarious ways,
Twisting and turning in colorful plays.

Each stroke a chuckle, each splash a cheer,
In this art world, we've nothing to fear.
With colors that jive and dance on the wall,
These paintings of laughter are made for us all!

So grab a brush; let's join the fun,
In this joyful gallery, we'll never be done.
A masterpiece made of smiles and dreams,
In the art of happiness, nothing's as it seems!

Chasing After Rainbows

Let's chase those arches, bright and bold,
With pots of laughter and dreams untold.
A silly dog wearing a rainbow wig,
On a pogo stick, dancing a jig!

Clouds are moody, puffed with glee,
While rain showers down, setting us free.
A parade of ducks in shiny galoshes,
Splish-splash their way, as they take their dashes.

With every step, a laugh we find,
As colors twirl and play, intertwined.
Painting the streets with a whimsical tune,
Chasing the rainbows, we'll be home soon!

So follow the giggles wherever they lead,
With a hop and a skip, we'll plant the seed.
A garden of laughter, blooming in play,
Chasing after rainbows, come join the sway!

Flora's Symphony of Light

In gardens bright, where daisies sway,
A tulip sings, finds words to play.
With leaves that dance on gentle breeze,
They laugh together, buzzing bees.

Petals paint the sky with cheer,
A daffodil whispers, 'Come, have a beer!'
Sunflowers chuckle in the sun's warmth,
While violets plot mischief, a delightful swarm.

Lilies twirl in a waltz so grand,
And roses tease with a gentle hand.
Each bloom's a note in nature's song,
In this symphony, we all belong.

Beyond the Rainbows' Edge

Past the arch, where sky meets ground,
A peach tree jests, with fruits abound.
Lemon drops tumble in playful rolls,
While orange giggles lift our souls.

There, a purple carrot tries to dance,
With broccoli beats, takes a wild chance.
Grapes do cartwheels, berries make jokes,
And dancing zucchinis spin with folks.

Ocelots wearing hats, oh so sweet,
Cabbage breaks into a two-step beat.
Each flavor, a laugh, a glimpse of cheer,
In this wonderland, nothing to fear.

The Luminescent Pathway

Glowworms gossip, lighting the way,
As mushrooms chuckle, night turns to day.
Crickets hum tunes in vibrant hues,
While fireflies wink, sharing their views.

A path of sparkles leads you straight,
To where every shade makes you feel great!
The moon's a lamp, shining so bright,
Tickled by stars, causing delight.

A rainbow-armed hedgehog starts to dance,
While lanterns sway in a merry trance.
Each step forward feels like a jest,
In this playful night, we are truly blessed.

Nature's Radiant Sonnet

Bees are poets with golden quills,
Crafting sweet lines, giving us thrills.
While ladybugs spin tales so bold,
In a theater where flowers unfold.

Every meadow's a stage for fun,
Where grasshoppers leap, their work almost done.
Butterflies wear costumes, vibrant flair,
Chasing their friends through the warm summer air.

Dancing daffodils, a vibrant tease,
Waving to daisies in the soothing breeze.
Nature's laughter fills this sweet spot,
A radiant sonnet, connecting each dot.

www.ingramcontent.com/pod-product-compliance
Lightning Source LLC
Chambersburg PA
CBHW072223070526
44585CB00015B/1468